Original title:
Path of Secrets

Copyright © 2024 Creative Arts Management OÜ
All rights reserved.

Author: Nolan Kingsley
ISBN HARDBACK: 978-9916-90-704-7
ISBN PAPERBACK: 978-9916-90-705-4

Quiet Revolutions

In the stillness, whispers grow,
Dreams awaken, futures flow.
Hearts beating, soft and true,
Change unfolds, anew we strew.

Voices rise in gentle song,
Together we learn to belong.
Light the path with every stride,
In this peace, our hopes reside.

The Undiscovered Fabric

Threads of gold in shadows weave,
Stories hidden, few believe.
Each stitch binds a silent tale,
Woven dreams that seldom sail.

Patterns speak in quiet hues,
Mysteries wrapped in subtle cues.
Unraveling the threads of fate,
In this cloth, we contemplate.

Secrets in the Moonlight

Moonlit paths where shadows dance,
Whispers echo, take a chance.
Every glimmer holds a clue,
Secrets waiting, old yet new.

Night unveils what day conceals,
Truths emerging, time reveals.
Underneath the starry dome,
We find magic, call it home.

The Lure of the Unseen

In the silence, wonders hide,
Gentle forces, deep inside.
What we know is just a part,
Of the world that stirs the heart.

Beyond the veil, the spirit sighs,
Inviting us to seek the skies.
For in shadows, light will gleam,
Catching glimpses of the dream.

Tales Under the Canopy

Beneath the leafy green, stories unfold,
Whispers of the ancients, secrets untold.
The breeze carries laughter, a soft, sweet song,
Echoes of the forest, where dreams belong.

Sunlight flickers gently, dappling the ground,
Nature's tapestry, where wonders are found.
Every shadow dances, every rustle speaks,
A symphony of silence, where the heart seeks.

The brook babbles softly, a tale of its own,
As branches sway lightly, in a rhythm unknown.
Creatures weave their stories, in harmony's thread,
A world full of magic, where fears dare not tread.

In this hallowed place, time seems to freeze,
Moments stretch like shadows, carried on the breeze.
Under the grand canopy, life feels so rare,
Each tale a treasure, wrapped in nature's care.

Threads of the Unseen

In whispers soft, the fabric weaves,
A tapestry of dreams and leaves.
Fingers trace the lines of fate,
Unseen threads, yet never late.

Across the dusk, in twilight's glow,
Invisible paths we seldom know.
Each moment stitched, a silent art,
Binding souls, though worlds apart.

Roads to Unwritten Stories

Beneath the stars, the pavement sighs,
Each road bears hopes, and quiet cries.
Adventures wait just out of sight,
In dreams that bloom, like flowers bright.

With every step, the tales unfold,
In shadows cast, and whispers bold.
The future calls, a beckoning tune,
In every corner, beneath the moon.

The Sigh of Shadows

In the stillness, shadows breathe,
They carry secrets, and gently seethe.
With every dusk, a story rare,
The sigh of shadows fills the air.

Behind each corner, silence waits,
A dance of echoes among the fates.
Embraced by night, their forms extend,
In twilight's grip, they twist and bend.

The Language of Secrets

Whispered notes in twilight's gleam,
A silent language, a hidden theme.
Words unspoken, yet deeply felt,
In corners where the shadows melt.

Between the lines, the truth resides,
In fleeting thoughts, where mystery hides.
Listen close, let silence speak,
The language of secrets, soft yet unique.

Echoes of the Unknown

Whispers dance upon the breeze,
Footsteps lost beneath the trees.
Shadows flicker, hearts entwine,
In the stillness, secrets shine.

Voices call from depths unseen,
Haunting dreams where we have been.
Echoes linger, memories fade,
In the twilight, truths are laid.

Veiled Footprints

Softly tread on paths concealed,
Mysteries in silence revealed.
Gentle whispers guide the way,
Veiled footprints, night and day.

In the shadows, secrets hide,
Past and present, side by side.
Follow where the shadows lead,
In their depths, our thoughts are freed.

Mysteries in Moonlight

Silver beams on water glide,
Secrets float on every tide.
In the glow, the world transforms,
Mysteries in quiet storms.

Softly gleaming, shadows play,
Nighttime's veil, a soft array.
Whispers wrap around the night,
Holding dreams in gentle flight.

The Silent Trail

Along the path where silence reigns,
Nature's whisper, soft remains.
Each step taken, echoes sigh,
In the stillness, time slips by.

Footprints lead to the unknown,
Winding paths where seeds are sown.
Through the woods, the heart will roam,
In the silence, we find home.

Tales from the Obscure

In shadows deep, where secrets lie,
Whispers curl like smoke in the sky.
Faded dreams in twilight's gleam,
Echoes of a long-lost dream.

Through ancient woods, the silence calls,
Where hidden hope and darkness sprawls.
Mysteries wrapped in cloaks of night,
Untold stories, out of sight.

Hushed Reverie

Beneath the stars, a gentle sigh,
In quiet moments, spirits fly.
Memories float like leaves resound,
In the stillness, peace is found.

Fleeting thoughts in silver light,
Dance softly through the endless night.
Eclipsed by dreams, the heart can weave,
A tapestry of what we believe.

The Secret Within

Deep in the heart, where shadows play,
A secret whispers, lost in gray.
Every breath holds tales so rare,
Unveiling truths beyond compare.

Hidden depths of soul's retreat,
Where silence wraps the bittersweet.
Glimmers shine through veils of doubt,
Unfolding what life's all about.

Labyrinth of Whispers

In winding paths where echoes tread,
Mystic voices softly spread.
Each turn reveals a glimpse of fate,
In twilight's hush, we contemplate.

Amidst the maze, a flicker glows,
With every step, intuition flows.
Secrets woven in a sigh,
In the labyrinth, we learn to fly.

Silent Revelations

In the hush of night, stars gleam,
Whispers dance in moonlit beams,
Secrets float on gentle air,
Silent truths we long to share.

In shadows deep, thoughts entwine,
Hearts reveal what eyes confine,
Echoes linger, soft and clear,
Silent revelations draw us near.

A breeze carries whispered dreams,
Flowing through the silent streams,
Nature holds its breath in awe,
Unlocking realms where we withdraw.

In the quiet, wisdom grows,
In every pause, a story shows,
Silent moments, softly spun,
Revealing joy when day is done.

Unraveled Threads

In the fabric of time, threads fray,
Stories linger where they lay,
Each pulled strand reveals the lore,
Of lives entwined, forevermore.

A tapestry of hopes unfolds,
Woven tales, both brave and bold,
With each knot, decisions sway,
Unraveled threads, in bright array.

Past and present, a delicate weave,
Truths emerge, hard to believe,
In every twist, a lesson sewn,
Unraveled threads, a path we've grown.

Through the eye of fate, we see,
The patterns of our history,
In this dance of fate and chance,
Unraveled threads invite the glance.

The Disguise of Dawn

Before the sun, the darkness sighs,
Shadows linger, in soft disguise,
Night whispers secrets, hushed and low,
Yet promise blooms in morning's glow.

With every hue, the world awakes,
Daylight paints, and silence breaks,
As colors burst from muted gray,
The disguise of dawn melts away.

Birdsong stirs the sleeping land,
Softly touching every hand,
Graceful light begins to rise,
Casting away the night's goodbyes.

In a moment, all transforms,
Awakening in gentle swarms,
The veil is lifted, dreams move on,
Revealing life, the new day's dawn.

The Secret's Embrace

In shadows held, a secret sleeps,
Nestled deep, where silence keeps,
A whisper wrapped in tender warmth,
The secret's embrace, like a charm.

With every glance, we dare to find,
Hidden truths that bind our minds,
In quiet corners, hearts will race,
Lost in the magic of secret's grace.

Moments shared, unspoken ties,
In glances thrown and fleeting sighs,
Every heartbeat, a gentle trace,
The world's soft pulse in secret's embrace.

When night descends, dreams intertwine,
Silent wishes, yours and mine,
In the twilight, love holds space,
Forever held in the secret's embrace.

The Enchanted Turn

In the woods where shadows blend,
Whispers call to hearts that wend.
Paths of light and dark entwine,
Where the stars and moon align.

A hidden door in ancient trees,
Opens softly with the breeze.
Mystic glows and secrets near,
Feel the magic, sense the fear.

Footsteps dance on autumn leaves,
Every heartbeat softly weaves.
Embrace the wonder, let it burn,
Find your way at each bend and turn.

Chronicles of the Concealed

In the shadows, secrets dwell,
Stories waiting for the bell.
Hidden truths that softly sigh,
Beneath the watchful midnight sky.

Pages turn in whispers tight,
Legends born from quiet night.
Echoes linger, fading fast,
And the silence speaks at last.

Unseen roads weave in the dark,
Guiding souls with a gentle spark.
Every tale, a flick'ring flame,
In the depth of mysteries' name.

The Unraveled Thread

A spool of thoughts begins to fray,
Life's tapestry, in disarray.
Threads of hope and fear entwined,
Searching for what's left behind.

Every stitch holds a story sweet,
Twisting paths where dreams repeat.
Hands unsteady, hearts anew,
Weaving tales of me and you.

With each pull, the patterns shift,
Frayed edges show the quilted gift.
In the chaos, beauty grows,
As the last unraveling glows.

Garden of Curiosities

Underneath the moonlit skies,
A garden blooms, where wonder lies.
Petals whisper, secrets lay,
In the night, they dance and play.

Fruits of knowledge, ripe and sweet,
Draw in wanderers on their feet.
Glistening paths of silver stone,
Guide the hearts that seek the unknown.

Every blossom tells a tale,
Of enchanted dreams set sail.
In this realm of endless quest,
Curiosity finds its rest.

The Maze of Unspoken Truths

In shadows cast by whispered dreams,
A labyrinth of silent screams.
Each turn a choice, each pause a sigh,
Lost in thoughts, as moments fly.

Beneath the weight of words unshared,
A tangled web of hearts ensnared.
The paths obscure, the signs unseen,
A quest for light, where hope has been.

Yet courage calls from within the night,
To seek the dawn, to find the light.
Through hidden doors, the truth shall gleam,
And free the spirit with a dream.

So wander forth, amidst the mist,
Embrace the shadows, persist, resist.
For every maze holds truths anew,
Awake the heart, and dare pursue.

Beneath the Surface

The stillness hides what lies below,
In depths where secrets never show.
Quiet waters, a tranquil guise,
Conceal the storms, the silent cries.

Each ripple speaks of tales untold,
Of dreams once bright, now dim and cold.
Echoes linger, whispers play,
As shadows dance in light's decay.

Beneath the calm, the currents churn,
In silence, hearts must twist and turn.
To dive deep down, where truths might dwell,
To face the fears, the hidden swell.

So brave the depths, embrace the dark,
For there you'll find the whispered spark.
From quiet seas, a world does rise,
Beneath the surface, wisdom lies.

Unfolding Mysteries

A riddle wrapped in twilight's grace,
Each moment holds a secret place.
With every breath, the world unfolds,
As time reveals what fate beholds.

The stars above, in silence hum,
Tales of the past, the unknown come.
In fragile whispers, stories weave,
As hearts draw close, and minds believe.

In hidden paths where shadows play,
The search for meaning guides the way.
With every step, the puzzles blend,
In the quest for truth, there lies no end.

So wander forth with eyes unshut,
Embrace the mystique, push and cut.
For in the dance of fate and chance,
The mysteries await, invite the dance.

Threads of the Uncharted

In tangled threads of life we weave,
The journey calls, we must believe.
With every step, a chance to roam,
To seek the sights, to find a home.

The uncharted paths, the roads unknown,
Are where the seeds of dreams are sown.
With courage as the guiding light,
We trace our steps into the night.

Each thread a tale, each knot a guide,
In this vast world, our hopes abide.
Embrace the twists, the turns ahead,
For every fear, a path we tread.

So let us journey, hand in hand,
Through lands unseen, through shifting sand.
For in the threads of fate, we find,
The beauty of the unconfined.

The Unseen Voyage

In the stillness of the night,
A ship sails without a sight.
Waves whisper tales of old,
Of treasures and dreams untold.

Stars above begin to gleam,
Guiding the lost on their dream.
The ocean cradles them tight,
As shadows dance in the light.

Silent winds carry a song,
Echoes of where they belong.
With every heartbeat, they roam,
Seeking a place they call home.

Through the fog, a path will gleam,
An unseen voyage, a shared dream.
Together they'll navigate,
The mysteries that await.

Legacy of Secrets

In whispers low, the past will call,
Echoed stories hidden in the hall.
A tapestry woven with threads of time,
Legacy cherished in rhythm and rhyme.

Letters faded, ink worn thin,
Revealing the truths buried within.
Each secret shared is a bond anew,
A thread connecting me to you.

Footsteps taken on ancient ground,
Hidden paths where love was found.
A treasure trove for hearts to hold,
In every tale, a piece of gold.

Guardians of memories long gone,
We tread softly as we move on.
In the silence, the past awakes,
A legacy that never breaks.

Whispers in the Twilight

As daylight fades to a gentle hush,
The world is wrapped in a muted blush.
A garden alive with soft sighs,
Where shadows meet the evening skies.

Crickets sing their nightly tune,
Bathed beneath the watchful moon.
Secrets linger in the air,
In whispers that we all can share.

Flickering stars begin to peek,
Adding magic, silent and sleek.
The twilight holds a sacred space,
For dreams to dance with timeless grace.

In this moment, all feels right,
Lost in whispers of the night.
A tapestry of dusk unfurls,
Connecting hearts and distant worlds.

Shadows Beneath the Oak

Beneath the oak, where stories dwell,
In hushed tones, a soft farewell.
Branches cradle the tales of old,
In their embrace, secrets unfold.

Leaves rustle in a gentle breeze,
Whispering memories among the trees.
Each shadow cast tells stories grand,
Of lives once lived, hand in hand.

The roots run deep, the past remains,
A guardian of joys and pains.
In silence, the oak stands tall,
Witness to the rise and fall.

Gathered here, in twilight's glow,
We honor the lives we'll never know.
In shadows beneath, we find a way,
To cherish the hearts of yesterday.

Unveiling the Obscured

In whispers soft, the truth does hide,
Behind the veil where secrets bide.
Flickering lights in the dimming night,
Unfold the tales of hidden plight.

As shadows dance on the ancient wall,
Echoes of past begin to call.
A journey through time with paths entwined,
Unlocking doors that fate designed.

The heart of darkness, a flicker of hope,
Each layer peeled, a wider scope.
Beneath the surface, let stories stream,
A kaleidoscope born from a dream.

So step inside, take a closer look,
Every chapter, a novel's hook.
With eyes unclouded, the world will glow,
In the light of truth, we learn and grow.

The Subtle Undercurrents

Beneath the surface, currents sway,
In silent whispers, secrets play.
Where thoughts converge in quiet streams,
The heart unveils its hidden dreams.

Like ripples forming on a serene lake,
An unseen depth, a tremor to take.
A pulse that hums in the silent air,
Threads of connection that linger there.

In crowded rooms, a glance exchanged,
An understanding, beautifully ranged.
The language spoken without a sound,
In subtle ways, our truths are found.

So listen close as silence breathes,
In every nook where nature weaves.
The undercurrents, both fierce and kind,
In every heart, a tale entwined.

Quiet Conspiracies

In hushed tones, the secrets rise,
A web of whispers, silent spies.
Trust is woven, a fragile thread,
In quiet corners, stories spread.

Beneath the smiles, a knowing glance,
An unspoken pact, a secret dance.
Plans are laid on the velvet night,
In shadows cast by the silver light.

With every heartbeat, alliances form,
In the stillness where dreams are born.
An echo of laughter, a stolen sigh,
Under the radar, the hopes fly high.

In tender moments, fate draws near,
A world built on trust, a bond sincere.
Each day unfolds like a close-held dream,
In quiet conspiracies, we gleam.

Shadows Speak

In the still of night, shadows creep,
With tales to tell, in silence deep.
They stretch and sway like ancient trees,
Whispering secrets on the breeze.

In corners dark, their language flows,
A dance of light, where mystery grows.
Through every flicker, a story shared,
In the twilight glow, truths bared.

With every flickering candle's gleam,
They echo softly, the dreams we dream.
In every shadow, a history dwells,
Of hearts once lost, and longing wells.

So linger a while with eyes closed tight,
Let shadows beckon in the moonlight.
In their embrace, the world feels right,
As shadows speak in the depth of night.

Illumination in Darkness

In shadows where silence dwells,
A flicker breaks the night,
Hope glows like distant bells,
Guiding lost souls to light.

Each whisper of the unseen,
Paints dreams on weary eyes,
In moments soft and serene,
Faith dances as it flies.

The darkest nights hold secrets,
Wrapped in a shroud of fear,
Yet courage often begets,
A spark that draws us near.

Within the void, a beacon,
Illumination calls,
In the depths, our hearts can reckon,
Love breaks through aching walls.

Maps of the Invisible

Beneath the waves of endless time,
Lies a map only few can see,
Tracing lines of thought and rhyme,
Where dreams intertwine with spree.

Each stitch a tale of lives once lived,
In places we cannot roam,
With every thread, the universe gives,
Paths that lead us back home.

The compass spins without demand,
As whispers guide the way,
We navigate the unseen land,
In shadows where visions play.

In the heart, a cartographer's skill,
Sketching roads yet unknown,
In every void, a beckoning thrill,
Mapping dreams where seeds are sown.

The Puppet Show of Truth

Strings of fate, they pull and sway,
As shadows dance beneath the light,
Wisdom weaves a grand ballet,
In a world that disguises plight.

Marionettes of every tale,
Play roles they cannot choose,
As secrets linger, pale and frail,
In truth, the heart can lose.

Curtains rise, and masks are worn,
Revelations spark the flame,
With each untold story born,
We grapple quietly with shame.

Yet in the chaos, a spark shines bright,
Truth's glow shall set us free,
In the puppet show, we fight for light,
To reveal who we can be.

Beneath the Starlit Veil

Beneath the vast, celestial dome,
Silent whispers rise and fall,
Hearts wander far from home,
Yet stars still heed our call.

In the quiet of the night,
Where dreams are softly spun,
Hope flickers, warm and bright,
A beacon for everyone.

As shadows blend with shimmering light,
The universe begins to sigh,
In stillness, we find our fight,
To reach for the boundless sky.

Underneath this starlit veil,
We gather strength to believe,
In the echo of each tale,
A tapestry we weave.

Crumbs of Concealment

In shadows deep, where whispers hide,
A trail of crumbs, secrets abide.
Each step I take, a tale to weave,
In quiet corners, I choose to grieve.

Beneath the surface, thoughts reside,
Masked in glances, nowhere to bide.
Fragments of truth, scattered wide,
In the heart's chamber, they quietly bide.

Memories linger, faint and pale,
Silent echoes unveil the tale.
In every shadow, a story glows,
Yet only to those who dare to pose.

So gather the crumbs, don't let them stray,
For in their puzzle, truths may lay.
Among the layers, one must seek,
The hidden heart that dares to speak.

In the Depths of Silence

In stillness deep, where shadows creep,
Secrets swim in oceans steep.
Words unspoken, a gentle flow,
In the quiet, truths begin to grow.

The heart will whisper, soft and low,
To those who pause, to those who know.
Beneath the surface, currents play,
And carry hearts in muted sway.

Each breath a tide, pushing and pulling,
In the void where thoughts are schooling.
Though silence reigns, it holds a weight,
A weight of dreams that won't abate.

So listen close, let silence speak,
For in that hush, the bold are meek.
In depths of calm, a storm can brew,
A world of wonders, waiting for you.

Hidden Currents

Beneath the surface, waters churn,
In hidden currents, lessons learn.
Flowing freely, yet unseen,
A dance of thoughts, in spaces between.

Waves of whispers, soft and deep,
Secrets rise and then they leap.
Carried forth by tides of fate,
In the silence, they gestate.

With every ebb, a story flows,
Past the harbors, where no one knows.
Seeking shores that hold the light,
In hidden depths, it feels so right.

So trust the currents, let them guide,
Through hidden ways, where dreams abide.
For in their sway, true strength you'll find,
In the spirit's flow, so unconfined.

Cloaked in Twilight

As daylight fades, the twilight reigns,
A gentle cloak, where mystery wanes.
In dusk's embrace, shadows intertwine,
Painting the world in hues divine.

The stars emerge, a distant blaze,
Whispers of night begin to raise.
In this stillness, magic stirs,
Time slows down, and silence purrs.

Beneath the veil, stories lie,
In twilight's grace, they stretch and sigh.
With every heartbeat, secrets bloom,
In the soft light, dispelling gloom.

So wander forth, 'neath twilight skies,
Embrace the dreams that softly rise.
In cloak of night, find solace sweet,
Where heart and spirit softly meet.

The Forgotten Lullaby

Whispers of dreams in the fading light,
A melody lost, in the still of night.
Crickets hum softly, cradling the dark,
While shadows dance lightly, a fleeting spark.

Echoes of wishes drift through the air,
Memories linger, a tender care.
Each note a promise, a sigh on the breeze,
A song for the weary, a heart's gentle ease.

Time slips away in a serene embrace,
As stars paint the sky in a silvery lace.
The world hushes softly, a breath held tight,
In the cradle of night, 'neath the moon's soft light.

Rest now, dear dreamer, let slumber take flight,
In the arms of the dark, all will be right.
A lullaby woven, a tale spun anew,
In the whispers of night, I sing just for you.

A Mist of Secrets

Veils of the morning, thick with the fog,
Hides all the truths in a shrouded dialogue.
Each step uncertain, on this hidden ground,
Mysteries linger where silence is found.

The trees stand watchful, with secrets to tell,
In the hush of the dawn, where shadows dwell.
Ripples of whispers, a breeze through the leaves,
Guide the lost traveler, who quietly weaves.

Dewdrops like jewels, glisten and shine,
Hold fragments of stories, both yours and mine.
In this misty realm, where dreams intertwine,
We find our reflections, so tender, divine.

Yet deeper we wander, through layers of gray,
Unraveling secrets that guide us astray.
With every soft breath, we uncover our fate,
In the embrace of the mist, we patiently wait.

The Unmoored Path

A winding journey, where time stands still,
Leaves drift like thoughts, in the autumn chill.
Beneath canopy whispers, I tread with care,
Each step a question, with answers laid bare.

Crisscrossing trails that beckon the heart,
In fields of gold, where the wildflowers start.
The horizon stretches, a canvas so wide,
I walk without fear, by the river's side.

With every new bend, hope dances in light,
Finding the courage to chase through the night.
The stars are my compass, the moon my guide,
On this unmoored path, I embrace the tide.

So let the winds carry my burdens away,
As freedom's soft echoes are here to stay.
This path yet untraveled, where dreams take their flight,
Is a journey of wonder, where all feels right.

Revelations in Twilight

In the hush of twilight, colors collide,
A canvas unfolding, with nowhere to hide.
Soft whispers arise from the night's gentle call,
As shadows reveal what the daylight would stall.

The horizon ignites in a fiery display,
Secrets come dancing, then drift away.
Each heartbeat a story, each moment a thrill,
Illuminated softly, beneath the night's chill.

Stars twinkle brightly, with wisdom to share,
In the embrace of the dusk, I breathe in the air.
The world holds its secrets, in silence they bloom,
As hope takes its flight from the closing of gloom.

So here in this twilight, I gather my dreams,
Let go of the burdens, unravel the seams.
With each revelation, my spirit takes flight,
In the magic of twilight, I am bathed in light.

Windows to Hidden Worlds

Through glass panes bright and clear,
Lies a realm held so dear.
Beyond the frame, stories twist,
In shadows and light, they coexist.

A whisper of dreams, soft and sweet,
Where time and space gently meet.
In vibrant hues, the secrets play,
In hidden worlds, life finds its way.

Each gaze reveals a doorway wide,
To wonders that ever abide.
In silence, the stories unfurl,
Windows to a colorful swirl.

A glimpse of fate in a fleeting glance,
Inviting hearts to take a chance.
With every look, new paths are found,
In hidden worlds, rich and profound.

The Forgotten Way

Beneath the trees where shadows reign,
A pathway lost, a whispering lane.
Once traveled by feet now gone,
The echoes of laughter linger on.

Footprints erased by time's soft hand,
In the stillness, memories stand.
Where dreams once danced in the sun's warm glow,
A testament to the paths we know.

Crumbling stones and wild vines creep,
Guarding secrets that nature keeps.
A journey traced in hearts that yearn,
The forgotten way may soon return.

Through tangled brush and the heart's own quests,
The path reveals what the spirit rests.
Find courage in the veiled embrace,
To walk again with gentle grace.

Furtive Glances

In crowded rooms, eyes fleeting meet,
A language spoken without a beat.
Hidden above, a story spins,
In corners dark, where intrigue begins.

A brush of fingers, a shared smile,
Moments captured, lingering awhile.
What secrets lie behind the gaze?
A world of wonder in subtle praise.

Whispers dance on the edge of night,
As hearts collide in the pale moonlight.
A glance exchanged, a spark ignites,
Furtive dreams take their daring flights.

In silken shadows, connections bloom,
Amongst the chaos, a quiet room.
Life's fleeting magic in stolen sights,
Furtive glances lead to endless nights.

The Serpent's Trail

In winding paths where serpents glide,
A tale unfolds, both dark and wide.
In coils and twists, secrets lie,
Beneath the earth and open sky.

Whispers in leaves, a silken sound,
Echoes of magic buried in ground.
With every curve, destiny speaks,
As ancient wisdom softly seeks.

Through tangled brush and shadows deep,
The serpent's trail, a promise to keep.
In nature's rhythm, life is unveiled,
In every turn, the heart has sailed.

A journey unfolds as fate entwines,
With lessons learned in silent signs.
The serpent winds, its path unfurled,
Guiding souls through a mystic world.

The Shrouded Road

In the mist where shadows creep,
The shrouded road, a secret keep.
Footsteps falter, silence reigns,
Lost in dreams, where hope wanes.

Beneath the trees, the whispers sigh,
Echoes of fate that linger nigh.
With every turn, the path obscured,
A heart once bold, now unsure.

Moonlit gleams through branches bare,
A flicker of light, a silent prayer.
Each breath an echo of things untold,
The shrouded road, a journey bold.

Whispers of the Ancients

In the stillness of the night,
Ancient voices take their flight.
Tales of yore in shadows dance,
Worlds entwined in whispered chance.

Ancestors' echoes call from deep,
Secrets held in time's dark keep.
A flicker of truth, a glimpse of lore,
Guided by spirits, forevermore.

They speak of love, of loss, of strife,
Threads of history, threads of life.
Eyes that witness, hearts that feel,
Whispers of ancients, ever real.

The Undertow of Truth

Beneath the surface, shadows swirl,
The undertow, a hidden world.
Questions rise like bubbles burst,
In the depths, a primal thirst.

What lies beneath the calm facade?
Veils of comfort, a cruel charade.
Dare we sink, or learn to swim,
In the undertow, truth grows dim.

With every pull, the current tugs,
A battle fought in unseen shrugs.
Face the depth, embrace the fear,
In the undertow, we draw near.

Within the Labyrinth

Twists and turns, a maze of fate,
Within the labyrinth, we contemplate.
Each corner hides a choice to make,
A fragile heart, a path to stake.

Echoes whisper, lost in time,
The pulse of moments, a silent chime.
Step by step, the shadows wane,
Finding light through twisted pain.

In the center, truths await,
Lessons learned, the end, or fate?
Within the labyrinth, we explore,
The journey's gift, forevermore.

The Cryptic Passage

In shadows deep, where whispers dwell,
A hidden path, a silent spell.
Each step I take, the walls confide,
Secrets kept, where phantoms glide.

Flickering light, a ghostly dance,
In ancient halls, the echoes prance.
Lost in thought, I tread with care,
A cryptic world, beyond compare.

Through winding turns, the air grows thin,
A mystery waits, where dreams begin.
The passage speaks in muted tones,
In crypt's embrace, I find my own.

Now shadows fade, yet still I roam,
In every turn, I feel at home.
The cryptic ways, forever call,
In the depths, I greet them all.

Tales Woven in Shadow

Beneath the boughs, where secrets hide,
Stories whispered, time's gentle tide.
The moonlight weaves its silver thread,
In every leaf, a tale is spread.

Ancient trees, with limbs held high,
Guard the wisdom of passersby.
In twilight's hush, the world concedes,
A tapestry of hearts and dreams.

Fables linger in the rustling ground,
Echoes of laughter, a sweet surround.
Each tale unfolds in soft refrain,
Woven together, joy and pain.

As shadows lengthen, they intertwine,
Lives interlinked, a sacred line.
In hidden glades, the stories grow,
Tales of life, in the soft glow.

Where Silence Speaks

In the quiet corners of the mind,
Where stillness reigns, and thoughts unwind.
A gentle pulse, a heartbeat's sigh,
In silence, truths begin to fly.

Amid the chaos, a hidden space,
Where echoes linger, thoughts embrace.
In the hush, the world slows down,
In the stillness, wisdom's crown.

Voices soft, like whispers feigned,
In solitude, the heart is trained.
Through silent paths, I find my way,
Where silence speaks, I long to stay.

Each moment held, a treasure rare,
In tranquil waves, thoughts lay bare.
Embrace the calm, let worries cease,
In silence, I have found my peace.

Moments in the Undergrowth

In tangled grass, where critters roam,
Life flits about, far from its home.
A hidden world, beneath my feet,
In every nook, a pulse, a beat.

Soft sunlight filters, shadows play,
Moments captured, they fade away.
In emerald depths, secrets reside,
Nature's stage, where dreams abide.

Fleeting glimpses of colors bright,
Wings of a butterfly take flight.
The rustle of leaves, a songbird's cheer,
Moments alive, forever near.

Through tangled roots, I journey deep,
In the undergrowth, memories keep.
Each breath a gift from earth below,
In nature's arms, my spirit grows.

The Fleeting Mirage

A dream drifts softly in the air,
Fleeting whispers, shadows bare.
Illusions dance in golden light,
Fading quickly, out of sight.

In the distance, forms appear,
But like the mist, they disappear.
What once was clear now blurs away,
In the twilight of the day.

Every glance a fragile thread,
Echoes of what might be said.
The heart yearns for what is lost,
In the quiet, we pay the cost.

Mirages haunt the soul's deep fight,
Promises wrapped in starry night.
Yet still we chase and still we roam,
For in the search, we find our home.

Signs Along the Whispering Way

Beneath the trees, a path unfolds,
With secrets held and stories told.
Leaves rustle softly in the breeze,
Carrying whispers through the trees.

Markers touch the sacred ground,
Messages in silence found.
Each bend and turn leads us near,
To the tales we hold so dear.

Footsteps echo, fading slow,
In the twilight's gentle glow.
Nature's signs, a guiding hand,
Lead us through this ancient land.

Let the journey find its way,
In the dawn of each new day.
For every whisper, every sigh,
Speaks of life, and love, and why.

The Veil Beneath

A shrouded world lies deep within,
Where shadows dance and silence spins.
Underneath the layers thick,
The truth awaits, both shy and quick.

In hidden realms of night and day,
Mysteries weave their subtle play.
Behind the veil, a pulse, a beat,
Whispers of life in shadows meet.

The heart knows well what eyes can't see,
Depths of hope, of fear, of glee.
In every tear, a story flows,
Of the veiled heart that truly knows.

So lift the veil and dare to gaze,
Into the dark, the light, the maze.
In every moment, every breath,
Lies the beauty found in depth.

Glimmers of Hidden Wonders

In the dark, a spark ignites,
Glimmers soft, like whispered nights.
Hidden treasures wait to shine,
In the spaces, yours and mine.

Amidst the chaos, find the calm,
A gentle touch, a soothing balm.
Every crack holds glories rare,
A universe beyond compare.

Look closely now, the world reveals,
Wonders wrapped in quiet seals.
In the mundane, joy takes flight,
As stars descend to kiss the night.

So seek the glimmers, chase the light,
For in the dark, it's within sight.
In hidden wonders, hearts may soar,
To places dreamed, forevermore.

The Darkened Corridor

Shadows loom in quiet halls,
Whispers echo, soft and small.
Footsteps linger, hearts will race,
Lost within this time and space.

A candle flickers, casting doubt,
What was here, and what's about?
Every corner hides a tale,
In this path where dreams might pale.

Silence reigns, a heavy veil,
Every breath tells a new tale.
Darkness deepens, flicker fades,
In the fear, the truth cascades.

With each heartbeat, secrets blend,
On this journey, will we mend?
Through the darkened, twisted night,
We seek solace, we seek light.

Secrets of the Forgotten

Buried deep beneath the stone,
Lies a truth that's not our own.
Whispers haunt the forgotten lands,
Lost in time, like shifting sands.

Ancient trees with stories old,
Guard the secrets they once hold.
Echoes linger in the breeze,
Carrying tales from ancient seas.

Faded maps and silver keys,
Unlock doors where memories freeze.
In shadows cast by flame's warm glow,
The forgotten yearn to grow.

Through the whispers, we begin,
To embrace what's held within.
In the silence, truths collide,
In the dark, the past resides.

Tides of Uncertainty

Waves crash gently on the shore,
Each retreat holds tales of yore.
What lies beneath the ocean blue?
Questions rise with every hue.

Currents pull, then push away,
Hopes that flicker, yet they'll sway.
Faces lost in shifting sands,
Dreams undone by unseen hands.

Tides of doubt and restless night,
Searching for a guiding light.
With each swell, we find our way,
Only time will hold the sway.

In the depths, where fears remain,
Brave the storms, embrace the rain.
On these tides, we rise or fall,
In uncertainty, live it all.

Echoes of the Mysterious

Footsteps light on paths unknown,
In dark woods where tales are grown.
Silent whispers weave their threads,
Haunting dreams and waking heads.

Stars align in cosmic dance,
Offering fate a second chance.
In the night, the shadows play,
Guiding hearts to find their way.

What lies waiting, just in reach?
Lessons hidden, fate will teach.
Mysteries wrapped in silver mist,
Moments cherished, never missed.

As dawn breaks, secrets fade,
Yet in hearts, the echoes stayed.
Hold the wonder, cherish sights,
In the dance of day and nights.

The Hidden Narrative

In shadows deep, stories reside,
Whispers of truth that often hide.
Pages unwritten, dreams unfold,
A tapestry woven, secrets told.

Through cracks in time, echoes ring,
Silent confessions of forgotten things.
Life's hidden beats, a subtle dance,
Unseen paths lead to circumstance.

Eyes may wander, minds may stray,
Yet the narrative finds its way.
Beneath the surface, hearts collide,
In the quiet, our souls confide.

Listen closely, let silence speak,
In the stillness, the brave will seek.
For every tale that lingers near,
Holds the weight of love and fear.

Lanterns of the Unknown

In the dark, where shadows blend,
Lanterns flicker, a guiding friend.
Mysteries dance in the night air,
With every glow, a secret to share.

Beneath the stars, the paths unwind,
Illuminating what we might find.
Each light a beacon, a promise cast,
In the realm of dreams that hold us fast.

Footsteps echo on the cobblestone,
Lost in thoughts, yet never alone.
With lanterns held, we brave the fear,
Through the unknown, the way is clear.

In every heart, a flicker burns,
Lessons learned as the world turns.
With every step, towards the divine,
We uncover fates that intertwine.

Footprints in Forgotten Dust

On dusty trails where echoes fade,
Footprints linger where we once played.
In the silence, memories bloom,
Whispers of laughter fill the room.

Time has painted memories grey,
Yet love remains in shadows' sway.
With each step, our stories trace,
A map of hearts in a forgotten place.

Beneath the weight of passing years,
The dust recalls our hopes and fears.
In the stillness, we find our breath,
A connection that survives even death.

With every footprint etched in time,
Life's rhythm pulses, a silent chime.
In the dust, our essence lies,
As we journey on, beneath the skies.

The Other Side of Silence

In the hush of night, whispers breathe,
Secrets draped like autumn leaves.
Silence carries what words can't share,
The unspoken thoughts that linger there.

In each pause, a world unfolds,
A treasure trove of truths untold.
Between the lines, emotions swell,
The language of the heart, so hard to quell.

Listening deeply, we start to see,
The other side of what it can be.
In silence, we hear the loudest calls,
The echo of love that never falls.

A canvas blank, potential bright,
In the quiet, dreams ignite.
For in the stillness, we may find,
The melodies that bind mankind.

Beneath the Surface

In waters deep and shadows cast,
Where echoes linger, memories last.
Secrets whisper, soft and low,
Beneath the surface, truths will flow.

The currents twist, the tides will sway,
Revealing dreams that drift away.
With every ripple, stories rise,
Beneath the surface, silence lies.

A treasure lost, a shipwrecked tale,
Of loves once bold, now faintly pale.
The depths conceal what hearts have known,
Beneath the surface, life is sown.

Dive deep within, where shadows play,
Unravel thoughts that fade away.
For in the quiet depths we find,
Beneath the surface, a deeper kind.

A Journey Uncharted

Wander far on paths unknown,
With every step, the seeds are sown.
Through forests dense and mountains high,
A journey uncharted, beneath the sky.

The stars will guide, the moon will glow,
As whispers of the winds will blow.
Each turn reveals a brand new dream,
A journey uncharted, like a flowing stream.

With courage held in open hands,
We carve our fate on shifting sands.
Each heartbeat echoes on this way,
A journey uncharted, come what may.

Embrace the wild, the unknown grace,
For in each moment, life we trace.
With every breath, a chance to start,
A journey uncharted, led by the heart.

The Undiscovered Way

Through tangled woods, the path is lost,
An undiscovered way, we dare the cost.
With every footfall, nature sings,
To hidden realms where wonder springs.

Beneath the boughs, in shadows deep,
Secrets stir and currents sweep.
Adventures wait at every bend,
The undiscovered way, our hearts extend.

With open eyes, we chase the light,
Through veils of mist, the day and night.
What lies ahead is yet unseen,
The undiscovered way, a vibrant green.

So onward tread, with spirits high,
Let dreams take flight beneath the sky.
For every step unveils a sign,
The undiscovered way, forever fine.

Masks of Enigma

In shadowed halls where echoes dwell,
We wear our masks, we forge our shell.
Each smile hides a thousand fears,
Masks of enigma, veils of tears.

In crowded rooms, we stand alone,
Afraid to show the heart we've known.
Behind each mask, a story waits,
Masks of enigma, woven fates.

The laughter rings, but deep inside,
The secrets bloom, we try to hide.
Yet every glance unveils a spark,
Masks of enigma, lighting dark.

But if we dare, let down the guard,
And share the truths, though they be hard.
In peeling back, we find the grace,
Masks of enigma, a true embrace.

Veils of the Night

Stars flicker softly, whispers in the dark,
Moonlight dances gently, leaving its mark.
Shadows stretch and sigh, secrets tightly spun,
In the deep of silence, the night's tale is begun.

The cool breeze carries, stories from the past,
Every rustle beckons, memories that last.
Neon dreams awaken, twinkling in the mist,
Veils of the night shroud, what we might have missed.

Ghostly figures wander, through the timeless haze,
Each step echoes softly, in a night's embrace.
The world is draped in mystery, cloaked sans fright,
Lost in the allure of the veils of the night.

The Tapestry of Concealment

Woven threads entwine, rich colors entwined,
Stories held in silence, in fabric defined.
Layers hide the truth, beneath the soft guise,
In the heart of shadows, deception lies.

Patterns weave together, a tale both old and new,
Each stitch a secret, known by but a few.
The art of concealment, a dance of the mind,
In the tapestry woven, the lost are confined.

Folded dreams linger, in each hidden seam,
Reality frays, unraveling the dream.
In this intricate dance, what's hidden shines bright,
Crafting the chaos, in the cloak of the night.

In the Garden of Shadows

Underneath the branches, where the sunlight fades,
Whispers of the twilight, in the cool of glades.
Petals softly falling, a carpet of despair,
In the garden of shadows, secrets lay bare.

Bees hum their ballads, as the night unfolds,
In the heart of silence, stories left untold.
The moon casts its silver, on pots of wild clay,
In this tranquil sanctuary, dreams gently sway.

Echoes of the past, dance through the air,
Haunting notes of sorrow, woven with care.
In the garden of shadows, time does not relent,
Each breath a reminder, of what was meant.

The Route Less Revealed

A path winds gently, through the misty trees,
Each step a question, carried by the breeze.
Footprints lost to time, on the ground below,
In the route less revealed, few dare to go.

Twists and turns await, in the thicket's embrace,
Hidden wonders linger, in this sacred space.
Every leaf that rustles, tells a tale to keep,
While echoes of the past, in shadows quietly sleep.

Adventure calls softly, with a voice like a song,
Daring the seeker, to venture along.
Finding joy in the journey, each moment surreal,
On the route less revealed, the heart learns to feel.

Labyrinth of the Unspoken

Whispers linger in the air,
Footsteps echo, unaware.
Shadows dance on ancient walls,
Secrets wrapped in silent calls.

Twists and turns, a winding path,
In the silence, feel the wrath.
Words unspoken hold their weight,
In this maze, we linger, baited.

Each turn hides a hidden thought,
In the quiet, lessons taught.
Breathe the silence, hear the dreams,
In the dark, nothing's as it seems.

Lost within the mind's embrace,
Searching for a sacred place.
Colors fade to muted tones,
In the labyrinth, we are alone.

Enigmas in the Mist

Foggy whispers roam the night,
Eager shadows, lost from sight.
Questions linger in the air,
In the mist, we're unaware.

Figures fade, then reappear,
Fleeting images bring fear.
Echoes of a distant past,
Through the haze, we drift at last.

Silent calls from hidden nooks,
In every glance, a thousand books.
Chasing answers left behind,
In the fog, we seek to find.

Enigmas spark our wildest dreams,
In the mist, nothing's as it seems.
Solving riddles one by one,
In the gloom, we chase the sun.

Starlit Secrets

Underneath the starry skies,
Whispers float like fireflies.
In the night, our hearts ignite,
Sharing secrets, pure delight.

Constellations tell a tale,
Of lovers lost and found, they sail.
Dreams reflected, shining bright,
In the starlight, we take flight.

Songs of cosmic harmony,
An orchestra of destiny.
Every twinkle, every gleam,
Holds the essence of a dream.

In the quiet, magic brews,
Starlit secrets, mine and yours.
With each breath, the mystery grows,
In this night, our love bestows.

The Forgotten Passage

In the depths of time, we find,
Paths once walked, now intertwined.
Whispers tell of ancient lore,
In the passage, we explore.

Dust collects on weathered stone,
Memories in silence groan.
Every step, a trace of fate,
In this journey, we await.

Echoing in chambers lost,
Time reveals the hidden cost.
Footprints linger in the dark,
Guiding us to leave our mark.

Forgotten stories, faint yet clear,
In this passage, we draw near.
Holding close what time has wrought,
In the silence, lessons taught.

Trails of Enigma

Footprints fade upon the ground,
In shadows deep, a mystery found.
Paths twist like whispers in the night,
I chase the echoes, seeking light.

Beneath the moon, secrets lie,
Stories told with a gentle sigh.
Nature's brush, painting the scene,
Life unfolds in threads unseen.

Winding through the silent wood,
Each step taken, misunderstood.
The heart beats in curious haste,
Another layer, another taste.

Puzzle pieces, edge and core,
Unraveling what came before.
In enigma's embrace, I dwell,
With every step, a tale to tell.

The Veiled Journey

A path obscured by morning mist,
Each breath taken, a whispered twist.
Footfalls echo, soft and low,
Guided by the sights below.

Veils of fog, they drift and sway,
Carrying dreams along the way.
In every shadow, stories lurk,
Secrets woven in the work.

The road ahead, uncharted lands,
Hope and fears weave in my hands.
With every turn, a heartbeat slow,
The veiled journey starts to flow.

Cloaked in wonder, draped in night,
Finding solace in the light.
The path reveals, the soul begins,
To dance with fate, where the tale spins.

Secrets in the Breeze

A whisper carried on the air,
Secrets woven, light as hair.
Rustling leaves, a gentle tease,
Nature's voice sings through the trees.

Every sigh, a tale to tell,
Of moments captured, lost in spell.
Dancing petals, drifting free,
Revealing whispered destiny.

In twilight's glow, mysteries blend,
With every gust, new paths will mend.
The breeze invites, if you dare stay,
To listen close, to what it'll say.

Unseen currents shape our fates,
In every breath, the world awaits.
Secrets come and secrets go,
In every breeze, the heart will know.

Echoes of the Unseen

In quiet corners where shadows dwell,
Echoes of the unseen swell.
A heartbeat waits, a caress tender,
In the silence, dreams surrender.

Whispers flicker like candlelight,
Unraveling truths hidden from sight.
Faint, yet clear, an ancient song,
Drawing hearts where they belong.

The tapestry of time weaves close,
In every moment, we find a ghost.
Shimmering threads that stitch our days,
In the fabric, love finds ways.

Unsung tales, they twist and meld,
In echoes deep, our souls are held.
To journey forth where shadows gleam,
To find the truth within the dream.

Whispers in the Twilight

The sun dips low, the sky ignites,
Beneath the stars, the quiet invites.
Soft echoes dance on the evening breeze,
Carried like secrets, among the trees.

Crickets sing their lullaby tune,
As fireflies waltz with the rising moon.
In this hush, the world fades away,
Leaving only dreams where shadows play.

The twilight whispers, soft and clear,
Tales of the night that we long to hear.
With every breath, the magic grows,
In the stillness, the heart truly knows.

Gentle night, with your velvet touch,
You cradle our worries, oh so much.
As whispers linger in the fading light,
We find our peace in the embrace of night.

Veils of the Unseen

In the depths of silence, shadows loom,
Mysteries hidden, waiting to bloom.
Glimmers of truth behind fabric and guise,
Veils of the unseen, where wisdom lies.

Whispers of echoes from days long past,
Secrets entwined, meant to last.
Layers of time wrapped in silt and dust,
Unravel the stories, as we must.

Through quiet corridors, we softly tread,
Following paths where no light has led.
With curious hearts, we seek and roam,
Finding the hidden, wherever we comb.

What lies beneath the surface so deep?
The dreams we cherish, the secrets we keep.
In the shadows, wonders are found,
Veils of the unseen, forever profound.

Shadows Beneath the Surface

Beneath the calm, the currents sway,
Shadows whisper, secrets at play.
Hidden depths where darkness flows,
A world unseen, where mystery grows.

Echoes linger in the tranquil tide,
In the empty spaces, fears abide.
Yet in the depths, beauty can thrive,
Where shadows breathe, and dreams survive.

Ripples dance over gentle waves,
Unlocking the stories the stillness craves.
Among the silence, hidden truths bide,
Awakening wonders, deep inside.

With quiet resolve, the heart will dive,
Into the shadows where we come alive.
For beneath the surface, we find our way,
Guided by whispers that lead and sway.

The Hidden Journey

Beneath the stars, we tread unknown,
Paths entwined, yet we walk alone.
With every step, the heart beats strong,
In the silence of night, we find our song.

Through valleys low and mountains high,
Chasing the dreams that never die.
A hidden journey, both far and near,
We gather strength with every fear.

In the labyrinth of our own design,
We seek the light, a thread divine.
Woven tightly into the fabric of fate,
The hidden journey, we contemplate.

As dawn approaches, the shadows recede,
Guiding our steps as we plant the seed.
For in every journey, the soul will learn,
From hidden paths, new insights, we earn.

The Shade of Meaning

In twilight's grasp, where whispers dwell,
Shadows dance, and echoes swell.
Each thought a leaf, the breeze does fight,
Seeking truths in fading light.

A silent path where dreams convene,
Amidst the laughter, a gentle sheen.
What lies within the heart's tight fold,
Stories untold, yet to be sold.

Glimmers shine through veil of doubt,
In the quiet, we find a route.
Resonance calls from deep inside,
In the shade where meanings hide.

Journey forth, for silence speaks,
In every crack, the wisdom leaks.
Dare to ponder, dare to grow,
In the shade, let meanings flow.

The Unfolding Mystery

Beneath the surface, secrets weave,
Threads of time, we can't perceive.
Each moment's gift, a soft surprise,
Layers deep, where wonder lies.

A fading echo from days of yore,
Calls us forth to explore more.
Each breath a chance to find what's lost,
Unraveling the dreams, no matter the cost.

In quiet corners of the mind,
Puzzle pieces intertwined.
Truths emerge on whispered breeze,
In the dark, the heart's unease.

As we wander through shadowed halls,
Mystery beckons, softly calls.
Embrace the dark, let knowledge light,
The unfolding mystery takes flight.

Journey to the Hidden Depths

In the stillness, silence sings,
A journey stirs, with hopeful wings.
Waves of thought pull us beneath,
To hidden depths, where dreams bequeath.

The ocean whispers secrets old,
Hiding treasures, brave and bold.
Each ripple's tale deserves a chance,
To dive in deep, to find romance.

Through currents swift and shadows thick,
The heart feels lost, yet finds the trick.
With every plunge, we gasp and yearn,
To seek the flame, to see the burn.

Underneath the mirror's guise,
Lies a world of thin disguise.
Journey on, the depths unveil,
In the dark, where stories sail.

Toward the Edge of Knowing

At dawn's first light, the world awakes,
A journey stirs, the soul remakes.
With every step, we seek, we find,
Toward the edge, our hearts aligned.

A chasm vast, a riddle wide,
Where shadows play and visions guide.
Each question posed, a bridge we build,
Toward the edge, our spirits thrilled.

In whispers soft, the truth resides,
Among the storms, where reason hides.
We tread the line of fate and choice,
Listening close, we hear the voice.

Through veils of doubt, we walk the now,
Toward the edge, we make our vow.
To seek, to learn, to always grow,
At the edge of knowing, we take flow.